KT-453-334

Pray Now
2000

Published on behalf of the
PANEL on WORSHIP
of the CHURCH of SCOTLAND
by SAINT ANDREW PRESS

First published in 1999 by
SAINT ANDREW PRESS
121 George Street, Edinburgh EH2 4YN

on behalf of the PANEL on WORSHIP
of the CHURCH OF SCOTLAND

ISBN 0 86153 281 3

British Library Cataloguing in Publication Data
A catalogue record for
this book is available
from the British Library

ISBN 0861532813

This book has been set in 10 pt Times Roman.

Book design by Mark Blackadder.
Illustrations by Sheila Cant.
Cover photograph by Walter Bell.
Printed and **bound** by H K Clarkson & Sons Ltd, West Calder.

Contents

Preface

TO know that we are part of
something greater than ourselves;
to offer thanks for goodness,
expected or surprising;
to seek the peace of all people and all things;
to claim renewing mercy –

these are great things to do,
great to permit their happening.

May this publication help in these directions.

Gilleasbuig Macmillan

CONVENER
PANEL ON WORSHIP
CHURCH OF SCOTLAND

Introduction

PRAY NOW for the year 2000 takes a somewhat different shape as the Panel on Worship felt that it was time for a change of format. We hope that our regular users will find the help they have been used to and more besides.

In some senses it is risky to change what has been, in the main, a very successful publication. Some might ask, Why change what is popular? The words and sentiments of the prayers seemed to have been well suited to those who have used it. Leave it alone!

The Prayer and Devotion Committee, who are responsible for producing the book, however, felt that there were good reasons for a change. One is that we can get too comfortable with any format. Like an old jacket or well-worn slippers, the 'comfortableness' of prayer requires to be disturbed from time to time, especially when we pray the familiar comforting words and are not aware of the One to whom we pray who communicates with us.

The second reason is that we are moving into a new millennium and are at the dawn of a new century. There is a sense that it is an appropriate time to change.

A third reason is that many people are wishing to explore different ways of seeking further intimacy with God. A renewed interest in spirituality has resulted in a plethora of books both Christian and non-Christian. Since it is the task of the Panel on Worship and its Prayer and Devotion Committee to aid the Church's prayer life, here is an attempt to help in the quest for a deepening of spirituality. In the Church, new and old traditions of prayer are being discovered and rediscovered.

In this book we have gathered together ways of praying that many find helpful today. A pattern of prayer for seven days is offered, but each person will fill this out in their own way, making use of the 'bank' of other material on later pages to enrich their daily prayer.

Here there is more choice, scope to adapt the material, room to experience new ways of praying. This book is not to be used 'from end to end' like its predecessor. Browse through it before you begin and find out all that is in store.

We present *Pray Now* in the hope that it will aid you in your prayer life.

Alastair J Cherry
CONVENER
PRAYER AND DEVOTION COMMITTEE

How to use
Pray Now

SHAPE OF THE DAY

Each day of the week
is based on a different theme:

Sunday: Creation
Monday: Birth and Incarnation
Tuesday: Suffering
Wednesday: Resurrection
Thursday: Forgiveness
Friday: The Holy Spirit
Saturday: The Church

SCRIPTURE SENTENCE

Each day begins with a Scripture Sentence based on
the theme for the day. Biblical quotations are from
the Revised English Bible, unless otherwise stated.

DAILY PRAYERS

There follows a prayer on the theme which seeks to
draw you into the presence of God.

BIBLE READINGS

Each day has a set of six readings from the Bible. You may wish to choose one or more of these, or you may follow a set of Daily Bible Readings – the choice is yours.

[A set of Daily Bible Readings is to be found on pages 65-78 of this book.]

SILENCE

Spend a short time in silence, maybe just a pause at first. Increase the period of silence each day as you wish.

PRAYER SUGGESTIONS AND ACTIVITIES

There are different ways of praying suggested in the book (see pages 20-52) which can be associated with the different days. Please try them!

INTERCESSIONS

Take time to pray for your personal concerns, community, national and international issues and the work of the Church of Scotland Boards and Committees. We hope that you might update these yourself as you learn of new concerns for the Church. Useful contacts are suggested which will allow you to have a more up-to-date prayer picture.

You may want to keep your own notebook of prayer concerns for this whole section.

LORD'S PRAYER AND BLESSING

Days of the Week

Sunday:
Creation

The heavens are yours, the earth yours also;
you founded the world and all that is in it.
(Psalm 89 : 11)

PRAYER

Creator God,
how precious are the moments
when your glory is revealed;
in the blush of the dawn of a new day,
in the song of the birds
as they praise you in their dawn chorus,
in the rainbow and the rain,
in the clouds,
one minute drifting,
the next scurrying across the sky.
Praise be to you,
in the quiet places;
by the burn,
on the mountain top,
in the forest,
in my own home,
by the fireside,
or some other special trysting place.
Thank you for precious moments,
when your presence is real
and I am left in wonder and praise;
in the gift of a new life,
newly born so complete;

in the laughter and tears shared,
in the light after darkness,
in the joy after pain.
Thanks be to you, O God.   *Amen.*

SCRIPTURE READINGS

Genesis 1
Genesis 2
Psalm 148
Isaiah 43 : 15 - 21
Romans 8 : 19 - 21
Mark 4 : 1 - 9

SILENCE

PRAYER SUGGESTIONS AND ACTIVITIES
(see pages 20 - 52)

PRAYER

Personal
The Local Community
National/International
The Work of the Church (see pages 53 - 57)

The Lord's Prayer

BLESSING

May God shield us in the valleys,
may Christ aid us on the mountains,
may the Holy Spirit bathe us on the slopes,
in the hollow, on hill, on plain,
mountain, valley, and plain.

(*Common Order*, p 597, no. 26, *alt.*)

Monday:
Birth and Incarnation

... Mary treasured up all these things
and pondered over them.
(Luke 2 : 19)

PRAYER

The pain and indignity of childbirth leads into
    the ecstasy of new life;
each new baby comes forth through trauma and
    anxiety;
each new day arrives after the long night.
Keep our hearts and minds open, O Lord,
to an awareness of new opportunities for living
    our lives in you.

Give us humility of spirit that we may be alive
    to new ways
and new opportunities for new birth and new
    growth in you.

Lord,
remember this day all who rejoice in the birth
    of a child.
Bless all new beginnings,
new relationships, new jobs, new opportunities.
May they all be dedicated to you.
Be very near to all who bring babies into a world
    of war, starvation and pain

Give them strength to continue,
and give us humility and purpose to help them
with our talents and money.
To you we pray, O God, the giver of life. *Amen.*

SCRIPTURE READINGS

Isaiah 9 : 2 - 7
Mark 1 : 16 - 20
John 3 : 1 - 8
Acts 9 : 15 - 19
Colossians 3 : 5 - 11
Revelation 22 : 17 - 21

SILENCE

PRAYER SUGGESTIONS AND ACTIVITIES
(see pages 20 - 52)

PRAYER

Personal
Community
National/International
The Work of the Church (see pages 53 - 57)

The Lord's Prayer

BLESSING

The guarding of the God of life be on us,
the guarding of the loving Christ be on us,
the guarding of the Holy Spirit be on us
to aid us and enfold us
each day and night of our lives.　　　*Amen.*

(*Common Order*, p 596, no. 23, *alt.*)

Tuesday: Suffering

Why should the sufferer be born to see the light?
Why is life given to those who find it so bitter?
(Job 3 : 20)

PRAYER

Where are you, Lord, when I am worried?
Where are you when I am in pain?
Where are you when I am at the end of my tether?

You are with me,
holding my hand, soothing my brow, giving me a hug.
My pain is your pain too.

Help me never to despair Lord, but to remember and
to know
that you are always with me, however bad things are.
Let me never forget that your everlasting arms are
underneath me.

I remember today,
all who suffer on their own
or on another's behalf.
May I be a messenger for you,
bringing love and peace to all those I meet who are in
trouble.

The world has its share of distress and sadness,
   O Lord.
May I never become hardened to the pain and
   suffering of others,
but always try to do what little I can to help,
knowing that I do it for you.
In the name of Christ who shares all our suffering.

Amen.

SCRIPTURE READINGS

Genesis 9 : 8 - 17
Psalm 121
Matthew 28 : 16 - 20
Mark 15 : 33 - 38
Luke 12 : 22 - 31
2 Corinthians 4 : 16 - 5 : 10

SILENCE

PRAYER SUGGESTIONS AND ACTIVITIES
(see pages 20 - 52)

PRAYER

Personal
Community
National/International
The Work of the Church (see pages 53 - 57)

The Lord's Prayer

O spring in the desert
O shelter from the heat
O light in the darkness
O guide for the feet
O joy in our sadness
O support for the weak
O Lord with us always
Your presence we seek.

Amen.

(David Adam)

Wednesday:
Resurrection

I am the resurrection and the life. Those who believe in me,
even though they die, will live,
and everyone who lives and believes in me will never die ...

(John 11 : 25)

PRAYER

Lord God
the night of darkness is over;
the grief and pain and uncertainty gone;
Christ suffered and died and rose again;
praise be to you for raising Christ Jesus.

When I am in doubt or despair,
    the presence of the risen Christ gives hope.
When I am in pain or distress,
    the presence of the risen Christ brings
        healing.
When overwhelmed by problems and difficulties,
    the presence of the risen Christ encourages.
When grieving or in sorrow,
    the presence of the risen Christ comforts.
When faced with challenges and risks,
    the presence of the risen Christ leads the way.
The triumph of the risen Christ removes all fear
    for death has been overcome.
Glory be to you, O God.   *Amen.*

SCRIPTURE READINGS

Jeremiah 18 : 1 - 12
Luke 24 : 13 - 35
John 20 : 19 - 22
1 Corinthians 15 : 1 - 11
Romans 6 : 3 - 6
1 Peter 1 : 3 - 5

SILENCE

PRAYER SUGGESTIONS AND ACTIVITIES
(see pages 20 - 52)

PRAYER

Personal
Community
National/International
The Work of the Church (see pages 53 - 57)

The Lord's Prayer

BLESSING

May God who is the ground of hope,
fill us with all joy and peace
as we lead the life of faith,
until, by the power of the Holy Spirit,
we overflow with hope.   *Amen.*

(based on Romans 15 : 13)

Thursday:
Forgiveness

For I know that my redeemer lives.
(Job 19 : 25, NRSV)

PRAYER

Merciful Father,
In day-light moments and night-time hours;
    I know that my Redeemer lives.
In brokenness and tiredness I come to you; for
    I know that my Redeemer lives.
I confess my inability to keep my word to you;
    yet still
    I know that my Redeemer lives.
When I am surrounded by the evidence of my
    weakness and sin;
    I know that my Redeemer lives.
When I want the earth to open up and swallow
    me whole because of what I have done;
    I know that my Redeemer lives.
When my mind revolts within me because of
    what I have thought;
    I know that my Redeemer lives.
At last I turn to you for help and comfort; for
    I know that my Redeemer lives.

At last I face up to what I am and what I am not
because
I know that my Redeemer lives.
At last I find and receive your gracious
forgiveness and mercy because
I know that my Redeemer lives.
Through Jesus Christ, my Lord and King,
my Redeemer who lives.

Amen.

SCRIPTURE READINGS

Psalm 103 : 8 - 18
Isaiah 62
Jeremiah 31 : 1 - 14
Luke 15 : 11 - 32
John 8 : 1 - 11
Hebrews 4 : 14 - 16

SILENCE

PRAYER SUGGESTIONS AND ACTIVITIES
(see pages 20 - 52)

PRAYER

Personal
Community
National/International
The Work of the Church (see pages 53 - 57)

The Lord's Prayer

BLESSING

May the eye of the great God be on us,
the eye of the God of glory,
the eye of the Virgin's Son,
the eye of the gentle Spirit,
the kindly eye of the Three be on us,
to aid us and to shepherd us.

Amen.

(Common Order, p 596 - 597, no. 24, alt.)

Friday:
The Holy Spirit

Suddenly there came from the sky what sounded like
a strong, driving wind ... flames like tongues of fire ...
coming to rest on each one ...

(Acts 2 : 2 - 3)

PRAYER

Spirit of God,
in stillness you brood over the earth,
in movement you sweep round the world,
in gentle breeze,
in driving gale,
in candle flame,
in blaze of fire.
Touching with tenderness,
challenging with passion,
unwearying in persistence,
unafraid in any circumstance.

Come, Holy Spirit, come wake within me the
    light of faith;
come, Holy Spirit, come rouse Christ's Church
    today;
come, Holy Spirit, come with joy in the morning
    and peace in the evening –

a dove to those in turmoil, an eagle to those in
    despair.
In the empty places of our minds and hearts,
    inspire us daily
and in the busy places of our lives,
    breathe calm and stillness for a moment.
Engage with us in daily living.
Walk with those whose journey takes them
    through corridors of power,
and spread your covering wings
    over this bitter-sweet world.
O Holy Spirit of God, hear our prayer.

Amen.

SCRIPTURE READINGS

Genesis 1 : 1 - 5
Joel 2 : 28 - 29
Ezekiel 37 : 1 - 14
John 14 : 15 - 27
Acts 2 : 1 - 13
Galatians 5 : 16 - 26

SILENCE

PRAYER SUGGESTIONS AND ACTIVITIES
(see pages 20 - 52)

PRAYER

Personal
Community
National/International
The Work of the Church (see pages 53 - 57)

The Lord's Prayer

BLESSING

With unflagging zeal,
aglow with the Spirit,
serve the Lord.

May the love of the Father enfold us,
the wisdom of the Son enlighten us,
the fire of the Spirit enflame us;
and may the blessing of God rest upon us
and abide with us, now and forevermore.

Amen.

(*Common Order*, pp 600 and 601)

Saturday:
The Church

With this great cloud of witnesses around us ...

(Hebrews 12 : 1)

Lord of the Church,
The place where we go each week to meet with
   you formally.
Not to tie you to one building
As if all the majesty and glory that overflows the
   heavens
Could be contained within four stone walls on
   earth!
   But our Church.
The place where life and death are celebrated.
   Our Church,
The place of baptism and new beginning,
Of family and growth; of learning and sharing,
   of singing and silence.
   Our Church,
The place of sermon and teaching, where your
   Word is faithfully passed on
For us to meditate upon, be challenged by,
   struggle with, puzzle over.
   Our Church,
The place where bread and wine remind us of
   that once for all event,

When broken body and spilled blood brought
    salvation to a believing world.
        Our Church,
Where marriage bells peal, and funeral bells toll.
        Our Church,
Where family and friends gather in the wider
    family.
        Our Church,
Where ancient songs and modern hymns
And flowers and fabrics
And tears and joy
Weave together to make the tapestry we know as
        Our Church.
Lord of the Church,
        Lord of our Church,
Lead us and bless us,
With the power of Christ.

Amen.

SCRIPTURE READINGS

Exodus 3 : 1 - 6
1 Kings 8 : 6 - 21
Psalm 100
Luke 4 : 16 - 21
Acts 11 : 19 - 26
Revelation 21 : 22 - 27

SILENCE

PRAYER SUGGESTIONS AND ACTIVITIES
(see pages 20 - 52)

PRAYER

Personal

Community

National/International

The Work of the Church (see pages 53 - 57)

The Lord's Prayer

BLESSING

May God make safe to us each steep,
may God make open to us each pass,
may God make clear to us each road,
and may he take us
in the clasp of his own two hands.

Amen.

(*Common Order*, p 597, no. 27, *alt.*)

Prayer Suggestions and Activities

Prayer Suggestions
and Activities

1: PRAYING IN EVERYDAY LIVING

THIS section is intended to help us make connections between ordinary activities and praying so that the two are integrated. Thus we can begin to discover for ourselves what Paul means by 'praying without ceasing' (1 Thessalonians 5 : 17). The Christian truths which form the pattern of the week have been used as themes providing creative links.

SUNDAY: Creation

We are used to thinking of Sunday as a day of rest. It is also helpful to think of this day as one for appreciating creation and creativity. Take the time to look at nature, and appreciate the life and vitality which is there. Reflect on and be glad about whatever creativity you take part in – whether it be craftwork, gardening, dancing, singing, and how these often link with looking after other people. Listen again to music you enjoy; look again at visual arts which speak to you. Spend some time to let these feed and nurture new life within you. The Creator God speaks in and through all creativity.

MONDAY: Birth and Incarnation

Ponder the new beginnings happening in your life at present: for example, a new family member – by birth, by marriage; new friends; life-changes for you or those close to you. Consider less obvious examples of birth in your life – like a new project at work; a new evening class; a book you are reading; a fresh understanding of God; a new interest; a new responsibility. Take a little time to offer any new beginnings to God. Reflect on how this gives new opportunity for the love of God to be experienced by you and those who share your life.

TUESDAY: Suffering

Take a moment to consider any suffering which is touching your heart today. Is it to do with your own life, the circumstances of a friend, a world situation which concerns you? Throughout the day, wherever and whenever it comes to mind, pray for that situation. You may find it helpful to picture the cross, or look at a cross, or hold a cross in your hand. This reminds us of Jesus from whom resurrection and new life come.

WEDNESDAY: Resurrection

God is always calling us onwards into new life, giving us more than we ask or expect. It is often hard to believe this because there is so much pain and suffering around us. Many daily occupations seem to restrict and limit new possibilities; yet the truth is that there is always new life. Treasure this new life as you move around today, keeping it in your mind and heart, walk with it. With every step you are walking with God into new places, new horizons.

THURSDAY: Forgiveness

Forgiveness is often associated with cleansing. Take a normal daily cleaning activity for you – for example, washing your hands, doing the family laundry, clearing your desk – and let that activity become a prayer. Speak to God as you do it, explore if there is anything making you feel 'dirty', 'uneasy' or 'unforgiven'. Allow the cleansing action to remind you of the depth of God's forgiving love, ever present for you to reach and draw upon, just in the same way as you are cleaning and clearing now.

FRIDAY: The Holy Spirit

The disciples had to wait for the coming of the Holy Spirit. Is there any area of your life where you feel as if you are waiting for God's help, wanting to discover God there, waiting to find guidance and direction, looking and hoping for God's renewing Spirit? Offer this experience of waiting to God and believe that in ways beyond your understanding there will be an answer or 'a next step' which will become clear. Live expectantly, yet without demanding an answer from God.

Traditional symbols of the Holy Spirit are a dove, wind, breath, fire. You can use these as a way of praying – letting your questions 'fly' to God; trusting that God will respond like the wind in unexpected ways; breathing in God's love and reassurance, breathing out your anxiety and worry associated with waiting; opening your heart to be enlivened and set on fire; or letting the fire of the Spirit burn up those things within you which hold you back.

SATURDAY: The Church

The Church is a place and a people of celebration. What is there in your life to celebrate? What is there in the lives of people you know to celebrate? The Church is where we come together with people we might not always choose. Ponder the wonder of God's love bringing us together, holding us together, helping us to appreciate the different gifts and personalities we all have. Pray for our own Church community. Pray also for the wider Church, this world-wide network which unites us. Let the food you eat, the books you read, remind you of the other parts of God's world and how we are all connected.

Prayer Suggestions and Activities

2: WAYS OF USING THE BIBLE

PRAYING THE BIBLE

This method of prayer goes back to the fourth century. Using a Scripture Reading as the base, it moves from reading to reflection, prayer and stillness in God's presence.

READING: Choose a short Scripture passage and read it slowly several times. Think about its setting, context, people and environment. What word or phrase speaks to you particularly?

REFLECTION: Spend some time (at least ten minutes) reflecting on this passage, perhaps repeating it to yourself a few times. How does it relate to your life, your situation, your relationships, your needs, your faith?

PRAYER: Use the issues, people and thoughts which have come to mind as the basis for your prayer. Prayers of forgiveness, concern or thanksgiving may spring from this. Perhaps take that text out with you into the day, repeating it to yourself during the day. As situations arise, reflect on God's word within them.

STILLNESS: Be still for a short time (or a long time) and welcome God's word afresh into your life.

As you read the passage, reflect on the symbols of which it speaks. The symbol may be 'light', 'water', 'fire', 'stone', 'mountain', 'oil', 'city'. It may be a religious symbol such as 'manger', 'cross', 'spirit', 'heaven'. It may be another related symbol or image that comes to mind inspired by the passage. Reflect on that symbol and what it means for you. Keep that symbol with you throughout the day and identify how it relates to your daily life.

Obtain an example of that symbol if appropriate and use it as your focus for prayer: for example, a stone, a candle (light), some oil.

FACE OF GOD

As you read the passage, which aspect or face or image of God is revealed to you: Creator, Healer, Parent, Almighty? Or think of the quality of God which is revealed to you: for example, patience, faithfulness, mercy, forgiveness, anger?

Allow that image or quality of God to be the focus for your prayer. Reflect on how that Face of God has looked upon you in your life. Reflect upon how you reveal that Face of God towards others. Go into the day and attend to how that image or quality is related to you or through you.

RE-WRITING

Re-write part of the Bible passage in your own words. Write as though you were there. Or you could write it in terms of your contemporary experience and circumstance. The Psalms are a good starting point for this.

This old-fashioned Sunday School method of teaching children the Bible is not only a method for enabling youngsters to win Bible exams. As you read a Scripture passage, notice which word or phase holds you. Memorise it. Repeat it out loud if you like. Take it with you into the day and repeat it to yourself. Notice how it affects your daily life. You could use the opening Scripture Sentence for the day.

Prayer Suggestions
and Activities

3: IMAGINING THE BIBLE

*This example can be adapted
for almost any Bible Story:*

READ: Luke 7 : 36 - 50
The woman washes Jesus' feet with her tears.

1: *Become familiar with the story*

Read and reread the story a few times until you are
familiar with it.

2: *Use the Relaxation exercise* (on pages 43 - 44)

3: *Entering the scene*

(a) Imagine the scene. You are going to be there, so
     try to get the 'feel' of the setting. Is it indoors or
     outdoors? Is it warm? cold? hot? stuffy? Is there a
     gentle breeze or is it still and calm? Feel the tem-
     perature, feel the breeze. What sounds do you
     hear? people? birds? animals? What are the smells?
     Take your time to experience the setting.

(b) Now put the characters in the scene. Perhaps Jesus
     enters the courtyard as the other guests recline on
     mats around the table. People are lying on their
     side to eat, resting on their left elbow and eating
     with their right hand – that is why the woman is
     able to wash Jesus' feet. Jesus joins them as guest
     of honour. How does Simon greet him? The feast
     begins.

     The woman arrives. What is the expression on
     her face as she sees Jesus and approaches him?
     What are the expressions on the faces of the
     others? Simon? Jesus? Listen to the conversation.

(c) Now move beyond the story. You are in the scene.
     How do you feel? Is there anything you now want
     to say to Jesus? If so, find an opportunity to speak
     to him. Do you want privacy or do you mind if
     others listen? Imagine yourself saying what you
     want to say to Jesus. How does he respond? Take
     your time. Jesus has time for you.

4: *Return and reflect*

When you are ready, reflect on what has happened.
Has it spoken to you about your life? Has it changed
the way you feel about yourself, about others, about
Jesus? It may help to talk through your feelings with
someone else, or to write your thoughts down in a
journal.

     You can use this procedure with a whole variety of
biblical settings. You can even revisit a particular
story.

Prayer Suggestions and Activities

4: REPETITION IN PRAYER

WE are used to repetition in some prayers. 'The Lord's Prayer' is repeated every Sunday in churches across the world. The response 'Lord in your mercy, hear our prayer' may be used several times in the course of a prayer. Repetitive praying is often misunderstood. It can have a depth and mystery about it which can allow us time to engage with and work through the words and images presented.

Often people enjoy singing Scripture choruses over and over, finding this very prayerful. The chanting of a sung response during prayers is very popular, such as 'O Lord, hear my prayer' (which comes from the ecumenical community of Taizé in France). Many in the Roman Catholic tradition discover a great strength in repeating 'Hail Mary, full of grace'.

Many people find using the words known as 'The Jesus Prayer' very meditative:

Lord Jesus Christ
Son of God
Have mercy on me
a sinner.

This simple prayer is easily learned. Its main purpose is to take your eyes away from a book and let the words easily flow through you.

As you sit with your eyes closed, repeat the lines slowly. Speaking them quietly at first can help. Let your breathing relax and find its own rhythm, then use the prayer a line at a time, breathing between each line:

> *Breathe in, breathe out*, Lord Jesus Christ, *breathe in, breathe out,* Son of God, *breathe in, breathe out,* Have mercy on me, *breathe in, breathe out,* a sinner, *breathe in, breathe out,* Lord Jesus Christ, *breathe in ...*

Each time you repeat a line, let a different image appropriate to that line enter your mind. You may find yourself focusing naturally on the word *Jesus*, or on the word *sinner*, or on the word *mercy*. It may be, and probably will be, different each time.

You may find that once you are more familiar with the prayer you will want to slow it down, perhaps even breathing after each word.

A number of easily remembered prayers can be used in this way. 'The Lord's Prayer' can take on a whole new significance for you when prayed like this. Or try it with words such as 'Father I adore you, lay my life before you, how I love you'.

Prayer Suggestions and Activities

5: PRAYING WITH EVERYDAY OBJECTS

A few examples:

1: *A CANDLE*

Begin with some relaxation or quieting down.

Light a candle and, if possible, sit in a darkened room so that some light is shed from the candle.

Look at the flame and observe the life that is in it. Watch its movement, brightness, and colours. Allow yourself time to watch the darkness and the shadows. Remember that light is itself a gift from God.

Think about the darkness in your life and watch the light. There is no need to try to solve any problems; it is enough to stay with the light for now.

Give yourself time to get in touch with the light of Christ shining in the dark places of the world. Stay with the light.

> *The light shines in the darkness and the*
> *darkness has never put it out.*
> (John 1: 5)

Remember Christ promised he would dwell in us. His light is within as well as outside you. That light is wanting to shine out through you and enlighten the world.

Think about the darkness in your life. Now think of yourself with the light of Christ shining through you. Pray for yourself and for others.

Think about the dark places in the world and the people there. Think of the light shining in front of you as you move around those places. Pray for them.

Before you extinguish the candle, pause to recall that the light will continue to shine within you. 'You who follow me,' said Jesus, 'shall have the light of life' (John 9 : 12).

2: A STONE

Select a stone, one you picked up at the seaside or from the garden. Hold it in your hand.

Look at the stone. Consider its colour, shape, beauty, and imperfection.

Think of where it came from … how it got there.

Now close your eyes and feel the stone … its smoothness … its roughness and sharp edges … its strength and weight.

Now in silence allow the stone to inform you:

- about creation;
- about the place where you gathered it;
- about what it says about your own life journey;
- about your own life –
    your smooth and rough edges;
- about your strengths;
- about your own beauty and colours;
- about how you support others;
- about your surroundings.

Think about God as your rock, and your refuge; think about yourself as a rock.

You can use the stone to symbolise the weight and burden of your worries. Then throw it away ... carefully!

Or place the stone in a position near your prayer corner, and let it remind you of God's strength, and of your own.

3: *A FLOWER*

Select a flower. Look at it. Reflect on it.

Its shape, colour and texture.

Close your eyes and smell it.

Think of where it was growing.

- Reflect on your own beauty and your own fragility.
- Reflect upon your own uniqueness.
- Reflect upon God's tenderness.
- Reflect upon creation, its diversity and its wonder.
- Reflect upon our abuse of the earth.
- Reflect upon ways in which you sully the world.
- Reflect upon how your life brings beauty to others.
- How might you care more for creation?

Place the flower in a vase to beautify your space and life. Give flowers to someone you love, or to someone who is ill.

Our lives are often reflected in the things we own and have around our home.

As you relax in your chair slowly, allow your eyes to drift around the room to the various objects, pieces of furniture, ornaments, pictures. Allow your eyes to pause at one. As you look at it, think about the occasion you obtained it. Was it a gift? something you bought with a loved one or on your own? a family heirloom? something made and given by a child? Is it beautiful? Is it useful?

If appropriate, think of the person associated with the item. Think of their relationship with you. Give thanks for the goodness experienced in that relationship. Remember that person in prayer.

Ask God to help you appreciate the people that you have now called to mind.

5 : *PRAYER ALBUM*

We all have at least one photograph album around our home, perhaps an old family one, or a wedding album, or some recent holiday snaps. Often they sit in a drawer or gather dust on a shelf.

Obtain a small pocket photograph album.
Gather together a few photographs which are important to you, such as of your family and friends.

Gather those special postcards which you never wanted to throw away because the picture is beautiful, or of a special place, or from a special person.

Gather those photographs or postcards you come across which simply attract you, or you find speak to you. The images on the cards may or may not be particularly religious.

Place them in your album, which now becomes your prayer book. It is not a tablet of stone, but by its very nature can change as you add to it, or remove from it.

The album can be used in various ways:

* In a relaxed position slowly look at the photographs and pray as each one encourages you so to do. Pray for the people in the photographs.
* As you look slowly through the images, allow God to speak to you through them. What is God saying to you?
* Create an album without people, but one containing other images which speak to you. It may be a Highland scene, a stained glass window from an ancient abbey, a statue, a reproduction of a painting, or an abstract image. You will soon have an album which is truly yours.

An Example of Praying
with Everyday Objects

- Select one image.
  You may choose it according to a theme, or it may be a random image.
- Relax in a comfortable position.
  Spend around ten minutes attending to the image.
- What does it represent for you?
  Does it arouse feelings of like, dislike, curiosity … ?
- Make some link with the image in a personal way.
  Ponder over it.
- After a time, close your eyes and dwell on the image and with all that it has come to mean to you.
- Allow your thoughts and feelings to direct your prayers.

Prayer Suggestions and Activities

6: PRAYING THROUGH OUR SENSES

PRAYER is not just a task performed in a certain place at a certain time in a particular posture. All five of our senses can be doorways into prayer if we use them attentively, because the whole of creation is shot through with the glory of God. Increasing our awareness during life's ordinary tasks can lead us more fully into the heart of God. If we are too busy, we miss so much, but if we attend to each moment, even when busy, we gain a great deal.

Here are a few ideas:

TOUCHING

If I can only touch the hem of his cloak
I shall be healed.

(Matthew 9 : 21)

- Attend to the moments when you are washing and drying your hands.
- Notice the textures of things you handle, allowing this to become thanksgiving: for example, clothes, wood, glass.

- Be aware of how you handle things.
  Do you grab or snatch?
  Could each touch be more compassionate?
- Make the preparation of food an act of thanksgiving.
  Hold and be attentive to the fruit and vegetables,
  and to the implements you use.
- How do you shake hands? How do you touch a
  loved one?
- How do you touch your children? Do you grab
  them when in a hurry?
  Can each touch be a blessing for them and for you?
- As you walk around the garden, the park, the sea-
  side, touch and hold things.
  Be aware of their texture, strength, fragility.

SMELLING

*Mary anointed Jesus' feet ... and the house
was filled with the fragrance of the ointment.*
(John 12 : 3)

- Stop to enjoy the scent of flowers, shrubs and
  herbs in your garden or in the park.
  As you pass a florist, take a few moments to
  appreciate the scents.
- Enjoy smelling your baby's newly washed hair.
- Give thanks for the aromas of baking from the
  kitchen.
- Enjoy the smell in the garden in the morning, or
  after it has been raining.
- When a smell takes your mind back to a childhood
  experience, give thanks.

TASTING

O taste and see that the Lord is good.

(Psalm 34 : 8)

- Attend to and appreciate the flavours of foods. Don't gulp down food without noticing.
- Don't eat and work at the same time.
- Eat out with a loved one or friend and enjoy the experience.
- A glass of wine shared can be an occasion of fellowship.
- Next time you receive the sacrament of communion, attend to the flavours and textures.

LOOKING

Their eyes were opened and they recognised him.

(Luke 24 : 30)

- Look at the faces of all whom you encounter today.
- Be aware of the expressions on the faces of your children, your loved one.
  Have another look at the colour of their eyes.
- Take time today to look carefully at the children's paintings and models.
- Do the images you usually watch on TV nurture you or depress you?
- Enjoy some of the photographs and pictures around your home.
- When you cut through fruit or vegetables, be aware of their colours, shapes and structures.

- Take a clear and attentive look at the flowers, trees and landscape around your home, and you may discover them for the first time.

LISTENING

Morning by morning God awakens me
to listen with a disciple's ear.

(Isaiah 50 : 4)

- First thing in the morning spend a few moments listening to the sounds, especially the birds.
- Be aware of the sounds around you during the day.
- Switch off the radio for a time and listen.
  What sounds are so often crowded out?
- Put on a piece of music and sit with your eyes closed and attend to it.
- Are you a listening person? A noisy person?
  Do you pay attention to what others are saying, or are you too intent on speaking?
- Go somewhere quiet and listen to the stillness. Hear what you often miss.

Prayer Suggestions and Activities

7: POSTURE AND BREATHING

Early in the morning ... Jesus went to a remote spot
and remained there in prayer.
(Mark 1: 35)

MOST of us will have our favourite seat in the house. Normally we will sit in the same position to watch television, or eat our lunch, just as we will sit in a similar place on a bus or in church. This familiarity enables us quickly to be at ease in our setting and posture in order to engage fully with the situation. A new position means we have to take time to accustom ourselves before we can begin to engage. It can be important to discover a place, a posture, an atmosphere, which enables our prayer life to be more focused.

Try out a few places, rooms, seats, lighting conditions, times of the day. Do not force something which does not work for you. If you have young children, then a quiet time in the morning will be well-nigh impossible. Perhaps you will have to find a time during the day or in the evening, when it is quieter and you have some time for yourself.

For some people kneeling is the most meditative position, and the use of a prayer stool can help to make this more comfortable. Many find the best way to read Scripture and pray is in bed at night. For most people a comfortable seat is best. Have your Bible and prayer books and journal (or whatever you normally use) within easy reach so that you can lift up and lay down without disruption. Put the answering machine on and volume off – remember to put it back on afterwards!

We can find it difficult to still ourselves for prayer. Our minds are usually so active. It can be very helpful to discover a way which enables you to be still and prepare for prayer.

Be comfortable. Find an open rather than a closed position: that means arms by your side or resting on your thighs, rather than folded across your chest; palms open and facing upwards or outwards, rather than clenched fists; head erect, rather than bent down towards your chest; feet apart and flat on the floor. Relax your body.

Listen to the sounds around you. Listen to the silence between each sound.

Focus on your breathing. Take some deep breaths. As you breathe out, release some of the tensions and worries. As you breathe in, become aware of God's Spirit which is the very breath of life.

Prayer Suggestions and Activities

8: HAND PRAYERS

ONE way of praying without words is by movement or gesture. We all know some prayer movements, yet rarely think of the movement itself as prayer. Simply to put your palms together is already a prayer without words. The movement expresses intention, direction of life, hope and trust in God. You can create your own prayers by using your hands.

Here are some suggestions to give you somewhere to start. There are seven which correlate with the themes for each day of the week. Use them as you find helpful. Experiment, adapt and develop them until you find what is prayerful for you.

SUNDAY: Creation

Sit and do nothing except be aware of all that is going on in your body. You breathe without thinking about it, your heart beats without your controlling it. Use your hands to help you be aware of your breath and your heartbeat. Feel the movement of your breathing by placing a hand or hands on the area of your diaphragm or abdomen. Feel the rhythm of your heart in many places – such as over or near your heart, the wrist pulse, the neck pulse. The natural rhythms can be very comforting. This is an experience that can lead to praise, wonder and worship, and can be a comfort when life around you is difficult, distressing, or agitated.

MONDAY: Birth and Incarnation

Start with the traditional prayer position of palms together at roughly the level of your heart. Begin with an awareness that your heart is where love is understood to reside, the place from which love is born. Open your palms to God with or without words. Realise that God is living and accepting you just as you are and is awakening new possibilities within you. Experiment with this gesture, repeating it in your own time.

TUESDAY: Suffering

Gestures can be used to get in touch with problems in our lives and then we can release them to God. The gesture of clenching and releasing our hands can be used in the following way. Think of a situation which causes you suffering, such as one that makes you anxious and tense, one that causes you pain and distress, or something which makes you angry. Hold this situation prayerfully and clench your fists. Gradually open your hands to release the tension, the pain, the emotions into God's hands, God's love, God's care.

WEDNESDAY: Resurrection

God takes us from where we are now into newness of life. Make this a prayer by moving your hands forwards as if they were feet going one step after another. Hold your hands at whatever level in the body is comfortable or meaningful, from your heart, from the area of your diaphragm, or from your abdomen. Experience the sense of being moved forward – pulled, encouraged, called into new things. Allow a prayer to come from within and/or hold in your mind a situation where you want God's help to enter into the unknown. If you have difficulty in any situation with moving on, ask yourself 'Where do I need Christ to help me keep going?'

THURSDAY: Forgiveness

Purge me with hyssop, and I shall be clean:
wash me, and I shall be whiter than snow.
(Psalm 5: 7)

Use a gentle face washing gesture as a way to help the reality of forgiveness suffuse your being. Even when we have said words of forgiveness in our heads, sometimes it is difficult to let the experience of forgiveness seep into our bodies and hearts. Find for yourself further movements that speak to your body and let you begin to digest the reality that God does forgive us, loves us, and offers us the gift of beginning again.

FRIDAY: The Holy Spirit

The Holy Spirit brings release, freedom, and energy for new life. The following movements can help you discover the reality of the presence of the Holy Spirit offering you freedom and lightness of spirit.

- Hold your hands together, closed but not clenched, and then open them as if you were letting a little bird free.
- Allow your hands (and your arms, too, if you want) to make a gesture as if you were flying.
- Open your hands and arms in a gesture of receiving.

SATURDAY: The Church

The Church is a place where we both receive from Christ and are drawn together with the family of God locally and internationally. Here we receive in communion. Try holding your hands in the form of a cup, and let yourself receive God's love. If it is meaningful for you, bring your hands to your mouth to imagine receiving the wine. Then let your hands move as they want to, giving praise and reaching out to others. Your hands may move to cover your heart, they may want to move upwards and outwards, they may want to open. Experiment with different possibilities and consider how much we use our hands to convey love and to build community.

SOME FURTHER COMMENTS
ON THE USE OF HAND PRAYERS

With these movements some people find it helpful to sing at the same time or play music which creates an atmosphere of prayerfulness.

Try using the movements for several minutes at a time, say five to ten minutes. Notice and reflect on any effects on your body, emotions, or thinking. Speak to God, most especially if you encounter resistance in yourself or difficulty in continuing with any of the movements. God accepts you with your inner resistance and any difficulties you find in receiving all the love that is being offered to you. Do not condemn yourself, but rather explore with God what you are learning about yourself. Ask and trust that the next step is being prepared for you to help you open up more deeply to the wonder of unconditional love – God's gift to each one of us. Remember that the movement itself *is* a prayer. There is no need for words, although they may arise spontaneously. What is important is that you get used to the experience that the feelings in the body can be themselves a prayer without words.

These gestures can be as meaningful through your imagination as actually doing them. So they can go with you wherever you are, even if you are in a context where it is not appropriate to express them physically.

It is often helpful to have someone you know to discuss and reflect with you the experience of this way of prayer. This provides an opportunity to say what you are learning and so deepen awareness of your own growth.

Prayer Suggestions
and Activities

9: PRAYING FOR HEALING

IT is often hard for us to know what or how to pray for those we know who are physically, emotionally or spiritually ill. It is also difficult to pray for ourselves when ill or to know how to ask other people to pray for us.

Here are some suggestions in addition to what you are already using:

1: There is a great comfort in knowing someone else is praying for you. People often find it helpful to know the time of day prayer is being made for them. Then it is as if you are tuning in with each other and God at the same time.

　　It can be very supportive to make a special commitment to pray for someone daily for a while, for example a week. The prayer may be a simple naming or 'holding' of someone else in God's love.

2: Imagine God's healing light in whatever part of the body is injured, and picture the body well and full of life.

　　You might find it useful to light a candle and concentrate on the flame. Let its light speak to you of the healing light of God which surrounds and is within us all.

You can pray in these ways for yourself as well as for others.

3: Sometimes when we pray, all the possible negative outcomes of the situation come tumbling through our minds.

In order to keep our minds focused on the beauty and wonder of God, try remembering a moment when you experienced God close to you.

You might choose to reconnect with a particular moment or a setting which speaks to you of God – a church, a favourite place, a sunrise or sunset.

Bring the picture of the person you are praying for into this remembrance of the wonder of God's love.

4: We all know that a gentle touch of a hand at the right moment can bring the reality of love and care to us.

You can do this for yourself.

Place your hands over the parts of your body which are suffering and concentrate on God's love, or repeat a Bible verse to yourself.

If it seems appropriate to do this for another person, check with them that they are happy for you to put a hand on them and make sure by keeping your eyes open initially to see if they are truly relaxed with your hands on them.

5: Music can bring healing.

Prayer can be singing.

Sing a song for the person for whom you pray, either with them or as you remember them.

For yourself, work out what music you experience as prayerful and set aside time to let the music speak to you of the ever present reality of God's healing love.

6: There may be occasions when one or two of you from your church are invited to support someone who is ill by visiting and praying with them.

You can use any of the above suggestions. There do not have to be words. What is important is to use whatever helps to keep your minds fixed on God. A vital ingredient in most healing is relaxation and calm for all involved. You can use any combination of the above suggestions with other material that is familiar to you. Ask yourselves what will help you to enable a 'healing space', a time when you feel the love of God bathing and surrounding you all with peace.

7: Another way of praying in twos or threes is for two of you to pray silently for the third person – listening, waiting upon God.

Then any of you may find coming into your mind a text, a word, a picture, like a message from God.

Offer the 'message', without any interpretation as to what it means. Through this, God can open doors to old hurts and painful memories.

As you speak and pray about them, commit the situation into God's hands. There can be much release, forgiveness and healing. If you are doing this, take turns to pray for one another and be prepared to be surprised by God.

Intercessions for the Work of the Church

TO cover the full range of the Church of Scotland's work, we are suggesting that you pray for the named Boards and Committees of the Church as well as their office-bearers. In some cases, up-to-date information can be found through special phone-lines or the newsletters and bulletins which are issued from time to time. The Church of Scotland magazine *Life & Work* can also be a useful source of information to help your intercessory prayers for the Kirk.

SUNDAY

The Board of Ministry
- in its work of recruitment, selection, education, training and in-service support of ministers, deacons and auxiliary ministers.

The Panel on Worship
- helping to refresh the worship of the Church.

The Panel on Doctrine
- wrestling with the meaning of the Christian faith for today.

The Committee on Artistic Matters
- concerned that the beauty and serviceability of church buildings should be such as will lead people to God.

The Board of Parish Education

- providing training for Christian discipleship and for leadership in the local congregations;

- those who hold the office of Reader, enabling the people of God to worship.

For up-to-date information on Parish Education matters see PEN, *available quarterly from the Board's publication section. (Tel: 0131-311 4704)*

Department of Education

- sharing Christian insights in the development of the curriculum and the design of courses, and helping shape effective religious education programmes.

The Church of Scotland Guild

- encouraging its members in their commitment to Christ and offering them opportunities for the active expression of their faith.

- Give thanks for the three year strategy 'Riches and Poverty', and its associated projects, now reaching its conclusion.

- Pray for its ongoing work, which for the years 2000-2003 will address the theme: 'Strength for Living'.

Up-to-date information on Guild matters may be found in the Newsletter *and* Prayer Calendar *produced three times a year, available from the Guild office.*
(Tel: 0131-225 5722)

Chaplains

- to hospitals, universities and colleges, industry, residential homes, schools and prisons – bringing both their needs and their insights to the attention of the Church.

The Committee on Chaplains to Her Majesty's Forces

- remembering its work with all who are involved in the armed services and peace-keeping forces.

The Board of Stewardship and Finance
The General Trustees
The Law Department

- resourcing the work and worship of the Church and guiding its affairs.

The Board of National Mission

- the work of the parish reappraisal and parish assistance committees and their concern that local churches are well staffed and well supported;

- the work of new charge development, remembering new and recently established congregations;

- the work of the Committee on Mission and Evangelism Resources;

- the work of the Scottish Churches Community Development Fund.

Up-to-date information on the work of the Board of National Mission can be found in Link Update. *(Tel: 0131-225 5722)*

The Society, Religion and Technology Project
The Iona Community
- both seeking to interpret the Gospel amid the challenges of contemporary life.

The Board of World Mission
- enabling our Church to share with, and be renewed by, Christians throughout the world.

  Up-to-date information on World Mission matters is available on their Update Line, *where details of personnel and locations are given. (Tel: 0131-226 4121)*

The Committee on Ecumenical Relations
- remembering the work of Action of Churches Together in Scotland (ACTS), Churches Together in Britain and Ireland (CTBI), Churches Together in England (CTE), the Conference of European Churches and the World Council of Churches, to all of which we belong and from whom we draw support.

The Scottish Churches Open College
- the ecumenical federation for Christian and adult education.

The Board of Social Responsibility
- working at the interface between Church and society, caring for those in need, and striving for the health of human community.

*Up-to-date information on Social Responsibility matters
is found in the* Circle of Care *newsletter available from
the Board. (Tel: 0131-657 2000)*

The Committee on Church and Nation
- giving voice to the Christian vision for our people
  and nation.

The Board of Communication
- working to make Church and gospel accessible
  through the news media, book and magazine,
  design, sound, film and Internet.

The Board of Practice and Procedure
- advising the General Assembly in its deliberations
  and decisions;

- the Moderator of the General Assembly, the
  Principal Clerk, and his colleagues.

The Nomination Committee
- ensuring that the Assembly's committees are
  resourced by people of experience and commitment.

The Assembly Council
- helping boards and committees together assess
  priorities, identify new challenges, and share
  resources.

The Personnel Committee
- caring for the staff employed by the Church.

Resources

Books

THERE are a large number of books, tapes, centres, retreat houses and courses available which focus on prayer and ways of praying as suggested in Section 2. Some of the books which have influenced the preparation of this book are listed below. There are also suggestions of resources which can aid and develop your prayer life.

Author: Henry Morgan
Title: *Approaches to Prayer: A Resource Book for Groups and Individuals*
Publisher: SPCK (1991)

* * *

Author: Angela Ashwin
Title: *Patterns not Padlocks: For Parents and All Busy People*
Publisher: Eagle (IPS Ltd) (1992)

* * *

Author: Anthony De Mello SJ
Title: *Wellsprings: A Book of Spiritual Exercises* (and other titles)
Publisher: Doubleday (1984)

* * *

Author:	David Adam
Title:	*The Edge of Glory*
	(and other titles)
Publisher:	Triangle, SPCK (1985)

* * *

Author:	Jim Cotter
Title:	*Prayer in the Morning*
	Prayer in the Day
	Prayer at Night
	Healing: More or Less
Publisher:	Cairns (various dates)

* * *

Author:	Gerald Hughes
Title:	*God of Surprises*
Publisher:	DLT (1985)

* * *

Author:	Dennis Linn, *etc*
Title:	*Sleeping with Bread:*
	Holding What gives You Life
Publisher:	Paulist Press (1995)

* * *

Author:	Agnes Sanford
Title:	*Healing Light*
	Healing Gifts of the Spirit
Publisher:	(Arthur James 1981/1979)

* * *

Author:	Russ Parker
Title:	*Healing Dreams*
Publisher:	Triangle, SPCK (1993)

* * *

Author:	Francis MacNutt
Title:	*Healing*
	(and other titles)
Publisher:	Ave Maria Press (1975)

* * *

Author:	Richard J Foster
Title:	*Celebration of Discipline*
Publisher:	Hodder & Stoughton (1989)

* * *

Author:	Gwen Cashmore and Joan Puls
Title:	*Clearing the Way: En Route*
	to an Ecumenical Spirituality
Publisher:	WCC (1990)

Retreats, Centres, Houses of Prayer

FIFE

Tabor Retreat Centre
Key House, Falkland KY15 7BU
(*Tel:* 01337 857705)

ISLE OF CUMBRAE

Cathedral of the Isles and
Collegiate Church of the Holy Spirit
Millport KA28 0HE
(*Tel:* 01475 530353)

EDINBURGH

House of Prayer
8 Nile Grove EH10 4RF
(*Tel:* 0131-447 1772)

GLASGOW

Ignatian Spirituality Centre
7 Woodside Place G3 7QF
(*Tel:* 0141-354 0077)

ISLE OF SKYE

Quiraing Lodge
Staffin
(*Tel:* 01470 562330)

PERTH

The Bield
Blackruthven House
Tibbermore PH1 1PY
(*Tel:* 01738 583238)

INVERNESS

The Coach House
Kilmuir
North Kessock IV1 3ZG
(*Tel:* 01463 731386)

Check *Retreats Handbook* for further listings (available
from the Scottish Episcopal Church, 21 Grosvenor Cres-
cent, Edinburgh EH12 5EE — *Tel:* 0131-225 6357).

Courses
and Networks

THE LIVING SPIRITUALITY NETWORK
and Newsletter

From Ruth Harvey, Director, The Well at Willen, Newport Road, Willen, Milton Keynes MK15 9AA. (*Tel:* 01908 200675)

SCOTTISH CHURCHES OPEN COLLEGE (SCOC)
Ecumenical Spirituality Programme

Annie Small Centre, St Colm's, 20 Inverleith Terrace, Edinburgh EH3 5NS. (*Tel:* 0131-332 0343)

THE CRAIGHEAD INSTITUTE

26 Rose Street, Glasgow G3 6RE. (*Tel:* 0141-332 2733)

Daily Bible
Readings

from Scripture Union – *Daily Bread*

NOVEMBER 1999

Mon	1	Exodus	39 :	32 - 43	❏
Tues	2	Exodus	40 :	1 - 16,	
				34 - 38	❏

Worship matters

Wed	3	1 Corinthians	10 :	14 - 22	❏
Thu	4	1 Corinthians	10 :	23 - 11 : 1	❏
Fri	5	1 Corinthians	11 :	2 - 16	❏
Sat	6	1 Corinthians	11 :	17 - 34	❏
SUN	7	1 Corinthians	12 :	1 - 11	❏
Mon	8	1 Corinthians	12 :	12 - 31	❏
Tues	9	1 Corinthians	13 :	1 - 13	❏
Wed	10	1 Corinthians	14 :	1 - 12	❏
Thu	11	1 Corinthians	14 :	13 - 25	❏
Fri	12	1 Corinthians	14 :	26 - 40	❏
Sat	13	1 Corinthians	15 :	1 - 11	❏
SUN	14	1 Corinthians	15 :	12 - 34	❏
Mon	15	1 Corinthians	15 :	35 - 58	❏
Tues	16	1 Corinthians	16 :	1 - 24	❏

Sing God's praises

Wed	17	Psalm	145	❏
Thu	18	Psalm	146	❏
Fri	19	Psalm	147	❏
Sat	20	Palm	148	❏
SUN	21	Psalm	149	❏
Mon	22	Psalm	150	❏

Jesus faces conflicts

Tues	23	Mark	11 :	1 - 11	❏

Wed	24	Mark	11	:	12 - 19	❑
Thu	25	Mark	11	:	20 - 25	❑
Fri	26	Mark	11	:	27 - 33	❑
Sat	27	Mark	12	:	1 - 12	❑
SUN	28	Mark	12	:	13 - 17	❑
Mon	29	Mark	12	:	18 - 27	❑
Tues	30	Mark	12	:	28 - 34	❑

DECEMBER 1999

Wed	1	Mark	12	:	35 - 44	❑
Thu	2	Mark	13	:	1 - 13	❑
Fri	3	Mark	13	:	14 - 27	❑
Sat	4	Mark	13	:	28 - 37	❑

Growing Christians: Christian victory

SUN	5	Romans	8	:	28 - 39	❑
Mon	6	2 Corinthians	12	:	7 - 10	❑
Tues	7	John	16	:	23 - 33	❑
Wed	8	2 Corinthians	2	:	14 - 17	❑
Thu	9	Revelation	19	:	11 - 21	❑
Fri	10	Revelation	21	:	10 - 27	❑
Sat	11	Jude			17 to 25	❑

David puts God first

SUN	12	1 Chronicles	10	:	1 - 14	❑
Mon	13	1 Chronicles	11	:	10 - 25	❑
Tues	14	1 Chronicles	13	:	1 - 14	❑
Wed	15	1 Chronicles	14	:	1 - 17	❑
Thu	16	1 Chronicles	15	:	25 - 16 : 7	❑
Fri	17	1 Chronicles	16	:	8 - 36	❑
Sat	18	1 Chronicles	17	:	16 - 27	❑
SUN	19	1 Chronicles	21	:	1 - 13	❑
Mon	20	1 Chronicles	22	:	2 - 16	❑
Tues	21	1 Chronicles	28	:	11 - 21	❑
Wed	22	1 Chronicles	29	:	10 - 25	❑

'Your Saviour is born'

Thu	23	Luke	1	:	26 - 38	❑
Fri	24	Luke	1	:	39 - 56	❑
Sat	25	Luke	2	:	1 - 7	❑
SUN	26	Luke	2	:	8 - 20	❑
Mon	27	Luke	2	:	21 - 40	❑

Solomon's dedication

Tues	28	2 Chronicles	1 :	1 - 12	❏
Wed	29	2 Chronicles	5 :	2 - 14	❏
Thu	30	2 Chronicles	6 :	12 - 27	❏
Fri	31	2 Chronicles	7 :	11 - 22	❏

JANUARY 2000

Turning the world upside down

Sat	1	Luke	3 :	1 - 22	❏
SUN	2	Luke	4 :	1 - 30	❏
Mon	3	Luke	4 :	31 - 44	❏
Tues	4	Luke	5 :	1 - 16	❏
Wed	5	Luke	5 :	17 - 39	❏
Thu	6	Luke	6 :	1 - 19	❏
Fri	7	Luke	6 :	20 - 36	❏
Sat	8	Luke	6 :	37 - 49	❏

Now is the day of salvation

SUN	9	2 Corinthians	1 :	1 - 11	❏
Mon	10	2 Corinthians	1 : 12 - 2 : 4		❏
Tues	11	2 Corinthians	2 :	5 - 17	❏
Wed	12	2 Corinthians	3 :	1 - 6	❏
Thu	13	2 Corinthians	3 :	7 - 18	❏
Fri	14	2 Corinthians	4 :	1 - 6	❏
Sat	15	2 Corinthians	4 :	7 - 15	❏
SUN	16	2 Corinthians	4 : 16 - 5 : 10		❏
Mon	17	2 Corinthians	5 :	11 - 21	❏
Tues	18	2 Corinthians	6 :	1 - 13	❏
Wed	19	2 Corinthians	6 : 14 - 7 : 1		❏
Thu	20	2 Corinthians	7 :	2 - 16	❏

Relationships: make or break?

Fri	21	Genesis	1 :	1 - 19	❏
Sat	22	Genesis	1 : 20 - 2 : 4a		❏
SUN	23	Genesis	2 :	4b - 25	❏
Mon	24	Genesis	3 :	1 - 13	❏
Tues	25	Genesis	3 :	14 - 24	❏
Wed	26	Genesis	4 :	1 - 16	❏
Thu	27	Genesis	6 :	1 - 22	❏
Fri	28	Genesis	7 :	1 - 24	❏
Sat	29	Genesis	8 :	1 - 22	❏

SUN	30	Genesis	9 :	1 - 29	❏
Mon	31	Genesis	11 :	1 - 9	❏

FEBRUARY 2000

Fix your thoughts on Jesus

Tues	1	Hebrews	1 :	1 - 14	❏
Wed	2	Hebrews	2 :	1 - 10	❏
Thu	3	Hebrews	2 :	1 - 18	❏
Fri	4	Hebrews	3 :	1 - 6	❏
Sat	5	Hebrews	3 :	7 - 19	❏
SUN	6	Hebrews	4 :	1 - 13	❏
Mon	7	Hebrews	4 : 14 - 5 : 10		❏
Tues	8	Hebrews	5 : 11 - 6 : 3		❏
Wed	9	Hebrews	6 :	4 - 12	❏
Thu	10	Hebrews	6 :	13 - 20	❏
Fri	11	Hebrews	7 :	1 - 14	❏
Sat	12	Hebrews	7 :	15 - 28	❏

God ... and evil

SUN	13	Psalms	5	❏
Mon	14	Psalms	6	❏
Tues	15	Psalms	7	❏
Wed	16	Psalms	8	❏
Thu	17	Psalms	9	❏
Fri	18	Psalms	10	❏
Sat	19	Psalms	11	❏
SUN	20	Psalms	12	❏
Mon	21	Psalms	13	❏
Tues	22	Psalms	14	❏

Belonging to Christ

Wed	23	2 Corinthians	8 :	1 - 15	❏
Thu	24	2 Corinthians	8 :	16 - 24	❏
Fri	25	2 Corinthians	9 :	1 - 15	❏
Sat	26	2 Corinthians	10 :	1 - 6	❏
SUN	27	2 Corinthians	10 :	7 - 18	❏
Mon	28	2 Corinthians	11 :	1 - 11	❏
Tues	29	2 Corinthians	11 :	12 - 21a	❏

MARCH 2000

Wed	1	2 Corinthians	11 :	21b - 33	❏
Thu	2	2 Corinthians	12 :	1 - 10	❏
Fri	3	2 Corinthians	12 :	11 - 21	❏
Sat	4	2 Corinthians	13 :	1 - 14	❏

An unrighteous country

SUN	5	Ezekiel	1 :	1 - 28a	❏
Mon	6	Ezekiel	1 :	28b - 3 : 15	❏
Tues	7	Ezekiel	8 :	1 - 18	❏
Wed	8	Ezekiel	9 :	1 - 11	❏
Thu	9	Ezekiel	10 :	1 - 22	
			11 :	22 - 25	❏
Fri	10	Ezekiel	33 :	1 - 20	❏
Sat	11	Ezekiel	34 :	1 - 31	❏
SUN	12	Ezekiel	36 :	16 - 38	❏
Mon	13	Ezekiel	37 :	1 - 14	❏
Tues	14	Ezekiel	43 :	1 - 12	❏
Wed	15	Ezekiel	47 :	1 - 12	
			48 :	30 - 35	❏

The good news of the kingdom

Thu	16	Luke	7 :	1 - 17	❏
Fri	17	Luke	7 :	18 - 35	❏
Sat	18	Luke	7 :	36 - 50	❏
SUN	19	Luke	8 :	1 - 21	❏
Mon	20	Luke	8 :	22 - 39	❏
Tues	21	Luke	8 :	40 - 56	❏
Wed	22	Luke	9 :	1 - 17	❏
Thu	23	Luke	9 :	18 - 36	❏
Fri	24	Luke	9 :	37 - 50	❏

Growing Christians: confident in Christ

Sat	25	Mark	2 :	1 - 12	❏
SUN	26	Mark	4 :	35 - 41	❏
Mon	27	Mark	6 :	30 - 44	❏
Tues	28	Mark	8 :	34 - 38	❏
Wed	29	Mark	12 :	28 - 34	❏
Thu	30	Mark	13 :	1 - 13	❏
Fri	31	Mark	16 :	1 - 8	❏

APRIL 2000

Abraham: faith in God's promises

Sat	1	Genesis	11 : 27 - 12 : 20	❑
SUN	2	Genesis	13 : 1 - 18	❑
Mon	3	Genesis	14 : 1 - 24	❑
Tues	4	Genesis	15 : 1 - 21	❑
Wed	5	Genesis	16 : 1 - 16	❑
Thu	6	Genesis	17 : 1 - 27	❑
Fri	7	Genesis	18 : 1 - 15	❑
Sat	8	Genesis	18 : 16 - 33	❑
SUN	9	Genesis	19 : 1 - 29	❑
Mon	10	Genesis	20 : 1 - 18	❑

Let us come near God

Tues	11	Hebrews	8 : 1 - 13	❑
Wed	12	Hebrews	9 : 1 - 10	❑
Thu	13	Hebrews	9 : 11 - 22	❑
Fri	14	Hebrews	9 : 23 - 10 : 10	❑
Sat	15	Hebrews	10 : 11 - 25	❑
SUN 16 [Easter Day]		Hebrews	10 : 26 - 39	❑

When darkness seemed to reign

Mon	17	Luke	22 : 1 - 23	❑
Tues	18	Luke	22 : 24 - 46	❑
Wed	19	Luke	22 : 47 - 71	❑
Thu	20	Luke	23 : 1 - 25	❑
Fri	21	Luke	23 : 26 - 43	❑
Sat	22	Luke	23 : 44 - 56	❑
SUN	23	Luke	24 : 1 - 12	❑
Mon	24	Luke	24 : 13 - 35	❑
Tues	25	Luke	24 : 36 - 53	❑

Abraham: God's promises fulfilled

Wed	26	Genesis	21 : 1 - 21	❑
Thu	27	Genesis	21 : 22 - 34	❑
Fri	28	Genesis	22 : 1 - 19	❑
Sat	29	Genesis	23 : 1 - 20	❑
SUN	30	Genesis	24 : 1 - 33	❑

MAY 2000

| Mon | 1 | Genesis | 24 : | 34 - 67 | ❏ |

Training in godliness

Tues	2	1 Timothy	1 :	1 - 11	❏
Wed	3	1 Timothy	1 :	12 - 20	❏
Thu	4	1 Timothy	2 :	1 - 15	❏
Fri	5	1 Timothy	3 :	1 - 7	❏
Sat	6	1 Timothy	3 :	8 - 13	❏

SUN	7	1 Timothy	3 : 14 - 4 : 5		❏
Mon	8	1 Timothy	4 :	6 - 16	❏
Tues	9	1 Timothy	5 :	1 - 16	❏
Wed	10	1 Timothy	5 : 17 - 6 : 2a		❏
Thu	11	1 Timothy	6 :	2b - 10	❏
Fri	12	1 Timothy	6 :	11 - 21	❏

Israel's boom-bust history

| Sat | 13 | Judges | 2 : | 1 - 23 | ❏ |

SUN	14	Judges	4 :	1 - 24	❏
Mon	15	Judges	5 :	1 - 31	❏
Tues	16	Judges	6 :	1 - 24	❏
Wed	17	Judges	6 :	25 - 40	❏
Thu	18	Judges	7 :	1 - 21	❏
Fri	19	Judges	11 :	1 - 32	❏
Sat	20	Judges	13 :	1 - 25	❏

SUN	21	Judges	14 :	1 - 20	❏
Mon	22	Judges	15 :	1 - 20	❏
Tues	23	Judges	16 :	1 - 31	❏

Watching and waiting

Wed	24	Habakkuk	1 :	1 - 17	❏
Thu	25	Habakkuk	2 :	1 - 20	❏
Fri	26	Habakkuk	3 :	1 - 19	❏

Praise God among the nations

| Sat | 27 | Psalms | 19 | ❏ |

SUN	28	Psalms	20	❏
Mon	29	Psalms	21	❏
Tues	30	Psalms	22	❏
Wed	31	Psalms	23	❏

JUNE 2000

Thu	1	Psalms	110		❏
[Ascension]					
Fri	2	Psalms	24		❏
Sat	3	Psalms	25		❏

Like Father, like Son

SUN	4	Hebrews	11 :	1 - 7	❏
Mon	5	Hebrews	11 :	8 - 22	❏
Tues	6	Hebrews	11 :	23 - 40	❏
Wed	7	Hebrews	12 :	1 - 11	❏
Thu	8	Hebrews	12 :	12 - 29	❏
Fri	9	Hebrews	13 :	1 - 16	❏
Sat	10	Hebrews	13 :	17 - 25	❏

SUN	11	Acts	2 :	1 - 4	
[Pentecost]				14 - 23	❏
				32 - 39	❏

Growing Christians: The role of the Holy Spirit

Mon	12	John	14 :	15 - 26	❏
Tues	13	John	16 :	4 - 15	❏
Wed	14	Luke	11 :	5 - 13	❏
Thu	15	Galatians	5 :	13 - 25	❏
Fri	16	Psalm	139 :	1 - 12	❏
Sat	17	John	7 :	37 - 39	❏

SUN	18	1 Corinthians	2 :	1 - 16	❏

Equipped for God's work

Mon	19	2 Timothy	1 :	1 - 7	❏
Tues	20	2 Timothy	1 :	8 - 18	❏
Wed	21	2 Timothy	2 :	1 - 13	❏
Thu	22	2 Timothy	2 :	14 - 26	❏
Fri	23	2 Timothy	3 :	1 - 9	❏
Sat	24	2 Timothy	3 :	10 - 17	❏

SUN	25	2 Timothy	4 :	1 - 8	❏
Mon	26	2 Timothy	4 :	9 - 22	❏

Secure in God

Tues	27	Psalms	15		❏
Wed	28	Psalms	16		❏
Thu	29	Psalms	17		❏
Fri	30	Psalms	18		❏

JULY 2000

Turning learning into action

Sat	1	Luke	9 :	51 - 62	❏
SUN	2	Luke	10 :	1 - 20	❏
Mon	3	Luke	10 :	21 - 42	❏
Tues	4	Luke	11 :	1 - 13	❏
Wed	5	Luke	11 :	14 - 28	❏
Thu	6	Luke	11 :	29 - 54	❏
Fri	7	Luke	12 :	1 - 21	❏
Sat	8	Luke	12 :	22 - 40	❏
SUN	9	Luke	12 :	41 - 59	❏
Mon	10	Luke	13 :	1 - 21	❏
Tues	11	Luke	13 : 22 - 14 : 6		❏
Wed	12	Luke	14 :	7 - 24	❏
Thu	13	Luke	14 :	25 - 35	❏

Chips off the old block

Fri	14	Genesis	25 :	7 - 11	
				19 - 34	❏
Sat	15	Genesis	26 :	1 - 25	❏
SUN	16	Genesis	27 :	1 - 29	❏
Mon	17	Genesis	27 :	30 - 45	❏
Tues	18	Genesis	28 :	10 - 22	❏
Wed	19	Genesis	29 :	1 - 30	❏
Thu	20	Genesis	29 : 31 - 30 : 2		
			30 :	17 - 24	❏

Power struggles

Fri	21	Genesis	31 :	1 - 21	❏
Sat	22	Genesis	31 :	22 - 42	❏
SUN	23	Genesis	31 :	43 - 55	❏
Mon	24	Genesis	32 :	1 - 21	❏
Tues	25	Genesis	32 :	22 - 32	❏
Wed	26	Genesis	33 :	1 - 20	❏
Thu	27	Genesis	35 :	1 - 21	❏

Refined by fire

Fri	28	1 Peter	1 :	1 - 12	❏
Sat	29	1 Peter	1 :	13 - 25	❏
SUN	30	1 Peter	2 :	1 - 10	❏
Mon	31	1 Peter	2 :	11 - 17	❏

AUGUST 2000

Tues	1	1 Peter	2 :	18 - 25	❑
Wed	2	1 Peter	3 :	1 - 7	❑
Thu	3	1 Peter	3 :	8 - 22	❑
Fri	4	1 Peter	4 :	1 - 11	❑
Sat	5	1 Peter	4 :	12 - 19	❑
SUN	6	1 Peter	5 :	1 - 14	❑

Wait for the Lord

Mon	7	Psalms	26	❑
Tues	8	Psalms	27	❑
Wed	9	Psalms	28	❑
Thu	10	Psalms	29	❑
Fri	11	Psalms	30	❑
Sat	12	Psalms	31	❑

Make every effort

SUN	13	2 Peter	1 :	1 - 15	❑
Mon	14	2 Peter	1 :	16 - 21	❑
Tues	15	2 Peter	2 :	1 - 10a	❑
Wed	16	2 Peter	2 :	10b - 22	❑
Thu	17	2 Peter	3 :	1 - 9	❑
Fri	18	2 Peter	3 :	10 - 18	❑

When all around has fallen

Sat	19	Job	1 :	1 - 22	❑
SUN	20	Job	2 :	1 - 13	❑
Mon	21	Job	3 :	1 - 26	❑
Tues	22	Job	4 :	1 - 21	❑
Wed	23	Job	6 :	1 - 30	❑
Thu	24	Job	9 :	1 - 35	❑
Fri	25	Job	11 :	1 - 20	❑
Sat	26	Job	14 :	1 - 22	❑
SUN	27	Job	15 :	1 - 35	❑
Mon	28	Job	16 :	1 - 17	❑

A good God

Tues	29	Psalms	32	❑
Wed	30	Psalms	33	❑
Thu	31	Psalms	34	❑

SEPTEMBER 2000

Fri	1	Psalms	35		❑
Sat	2	Psalms	36		❑
SUN	3	Psalms	37		❑

When you just don't understand

Mon	4	Job	19 :	1 - 29	❑
Tues	5	Job	23 :	1 - 24 : 1	❑
Wed	6	Job	28 :	1 - 28	❑
Thu	7	Job	29 :	1 - 25	❑
Fri	8	Job	32 :	1 - 22	❑
Sat	9	Job	33 :	1 - 33	❑
SUN	10	Job	38 :	1 - 30	❑
Mon	11	Job	40 :	1 - 24	❑
Tues	12	Job	42 :	1 - 17	❑

A woman after God's own heart

Wed	13	Ruth	1 :	1 - 22	❑
Thu	14	Ruth	2 :	1 - 23	❑
Fri	15	Ruth	3 :	1 - 18	❑
Sat	16	Ruth	4 :	1 - 22	❑

Growing Christians: knowing God's will

SUN	17	Psalms	25 :	4 - 10	❑
Mon	18	Psalms	32 :	1 - 11	❑
Tues	19	Psalms	40 :	1 - 11	❑
Wed	20	Psalms	119 :	1 - 32	❑
Thu	21	Proverbs	3 :	1 - 18	❑
Fri	22	Proverbs	3 :	19 - 35	❑
Sat	23	Proverbs	16 :	1 - 9	❑

Lost and found

SUN	24	Luke	15 :	1 - 10	❑
Mon	25	Luke	15 :	11 - 32	❑
Tues	26	Luke	16 :	1 - 13	❑
Wed	27	Luke	16 :	14 - 31	❑
Thu	28	Luke	17 :	1 - 19	❑
Fri	29	Luke	17 :	20 - 37	❑
Sat	30	Luke	18 :	1 - 14	❑

OCTOBER 2000

Building up the body of Christ

SUN	1	Ephesians	1 :	1 - 14	❑
Mon	2	Ephesians	1 :	15 - 23	❑
Tues	3	Ephesians	2 :	1 - 10	❑
Wed	4	Ephesians	2 :	11 - 22	❑
Thu	5	Ephesians	3 :	1 - 13	❑
Fri	6	Ephesians	3 :	14 - 21	❑
Sat	7	Ephesians	4 :	1 - 6	❑
SUN	8	Ephesians	4 :	7 - 16	❑
Mon	9	Ephesians	4 :	17 - 32	❑
Tues	10	Ephesians	5 :	1 - 20	❑
Wed	11	Ephesians	5 :	21 - 33	❑
Thu	12	Ephesians	6 :	1 - 9	❑
Fri	13	Ephesians	6 :	10 - 24	

Joseph: a rising star

Sat	14	Genesis	37 :	1 - 11	❑
SUN	15	Genesis	37 :	12 - 36	❑
Mon	16	Genesis	39 :	1 - 23	❑
Tues	17	Genesis	40 :	1 - 23	❑
Wed	18	Genesis	41 :	1 - 36	❑
Thu	19	Genesis	41 :	37 - 57	❑

Working towards reconciliation

Fri	20	Genesis	42 :	1 - 24	❑
Sat	21	Genesis	42 :	25 - 38	❑
SUN	22	Genesis	43 :	1 - 34	❑
Mon	23	Genesis	44 :	1 - 34	❑
Tues	24	Genesis	45 :	1 - 28	❑
Wed	25	Genesis	46 :	1 - 27	❑
Thu	26	Genesis	46 : 28 - 47 : 12		❑
Fri	27	Genesis	47 :	13 - 31	❑
Sat	28	Genesis	48 :	1 - 22	❑
SUN	29	Genesis	49 :	1 - 13	❑
Mon	30	Genesis	49 :	14 - 28	❑
Tues	31	Genesis	49 : 29 - 50 : 14		❑

NOVEMBER 2000

Wed	1	Genesis	50 :	15 - 26	❏

Responding to Jesus

Thu	2	Luke	18 :	15 - 30	❏
Fri	3	Luke	18 :	31 - 43	❏
Sat	4	Luke	19 :	1 - 10	❏
SUN	5	Luke	19 :	11 - 27	❏
Mon	6	Luke	19 :	28 - 48	❏
Tues	7	Luke	20 :	1 - 18	❏
Wed	8	Luke	20 :	19 - 47	❏
Thu	9	Luke	21 :	1 - 19	❏
Fri	10	Luke	21 :	20 - 38	❏

Wrestling with God

Sat	11	Psalms	38		❏
SUN	12	Psalms	39		❏
Mon	13	Psalms	40		❏
Tues	14	Psalms	41		❏
Wed	15	Psalms	42		❏
Thu	16	Psalms	43		❏
Fri	17	Psalms	44		❏

Listening and doing

Sat	18	James	1 :	1 - 11	❏
SUN	19	James	1 :	12 - 18	❏
Mon	20	James	1 :	19 - 27	❏
Tues	21	James	2 :	1 - 13	❏
Wed	22	James	2 :	14 - 26	❏
Thu	23	James	3 :	1 - 12	❏
Fri	24	James	3 :	13 - 18	❏
Sat	25	James	4 :	1 - 10	❏
SUN	26	James	4 :	11 - 17	❏
Mon	27	James	5 :	1 - 6	❏
Tues	28	James	5 :	7 - 20	❏

Israel: the next generation

Wed	29	Joshua	1 :	1 - 18	❏
Thu	30	Joshua	2 :	1 - 24	❏

Fri	1	Joshua	3	:	1 - 17	❏
Sat	2	Joshua	4	: 1 - 5 :	1	❏
SUN	3	Joshua	5	:	2 - 15	❏
Mon	4	Joshua	6	:	1 - 27	❏
Tues	5	Joshua	7	:	1 - 26	❏
Wed	6	Joshua	8	:	1 - 29	❏
Thu	7	Joshua	14	:	6 - 15	❏
Fri	8	Joshua	20	:	1 - 9	❏
Sat	9	Joshua	23	:	1 - 16	❏
SUN	10	Joshua	24	:	1 - 15	❏
Mon	11	Joshua	24	:	16 - 23	❏

Growing Christians: Jesus – God and man

Tues	12	Romans	1	:	1 - 7	❏
Wed	13	John	1	:	1 - 5	❏
Thu	14	John	1	:	9 - 18	❏
Fri	15	Hebrews	10	:	1 - 10	❏
Sat	16	Hebrews	2	:	1 - 18	❏
SUN	17	Philippians	3	:	1 - 21	❏
Mon	18	Philippians	2	:	1 - 30	❏

Mission impossible: saving the human race

Tues	19	Luke	1	:	1 - 25	❏
Wed	20	Luke	1	:	26 - 38	❏
Thu	21	Luke	1	:	39 - 45	❏
Fri	22	Luke	1	:	46 - 56	❏
Sat	23	Luke	1	:	57 - 66	❏
SUN	24	Luke	1	:	67 - 80	❏
Mon	25	Luke	2	:	1 - 20	❏
Tues	26	Luke	2	:	21 - 38	❏
Wed	27	Luke	2	:	39 - 52	❏

Mercy and discipline

Thu	28	Jonah	1	:	1 - 17	❏
Fri	29	Jonah	2	:	1 - 10	❏
Sat	30	Jonah	3	:	1 - 10	❏
SUN	31	Jonah	4	:	1 - 11	❏

Acknowledgements

SCRIPTURAL quotations, with one exception, are from the *Revised English Bible* © Oxford University Press and Cambridge University Press 1989 and are reproduced by permission.

The Scripture Sentence for Thursday is from the *New Revised Standard Version* and is reproduced by permission of the Division of Christian Education of the National Council of the Churches of Christ in the United States of America.

The Blessing for Tuesday, 'O spring in the desert', is from *Tides and Seasons* by David Adam (London: SPCK) and is reproduced by permission.

The list of Daily Bible Readings is from *Daily Bread* and is reproduced by kind permission of Scripture Union (Scotland), 9 Canal Street, Glasgow G4 0AD.

Pray Now was prepared by members of the Panel on Worship's Prayer and Devotion Committee: Derek Browning, Alastair Cherry, Greta Doig, Diana Lamb, Stewart McPherson, Margaret Millar, Laura Shepherd, Jenny Williams.

For further information about *Pray Now* and other publications from the Panel on Worship, contact:

Office for Worship
Church of Scotland
121 George Street
EDINBURGH EH2 4YN
(*Tel:* 0131-225 5722)
(*Fax:* 0131-220 3113)